I0605465

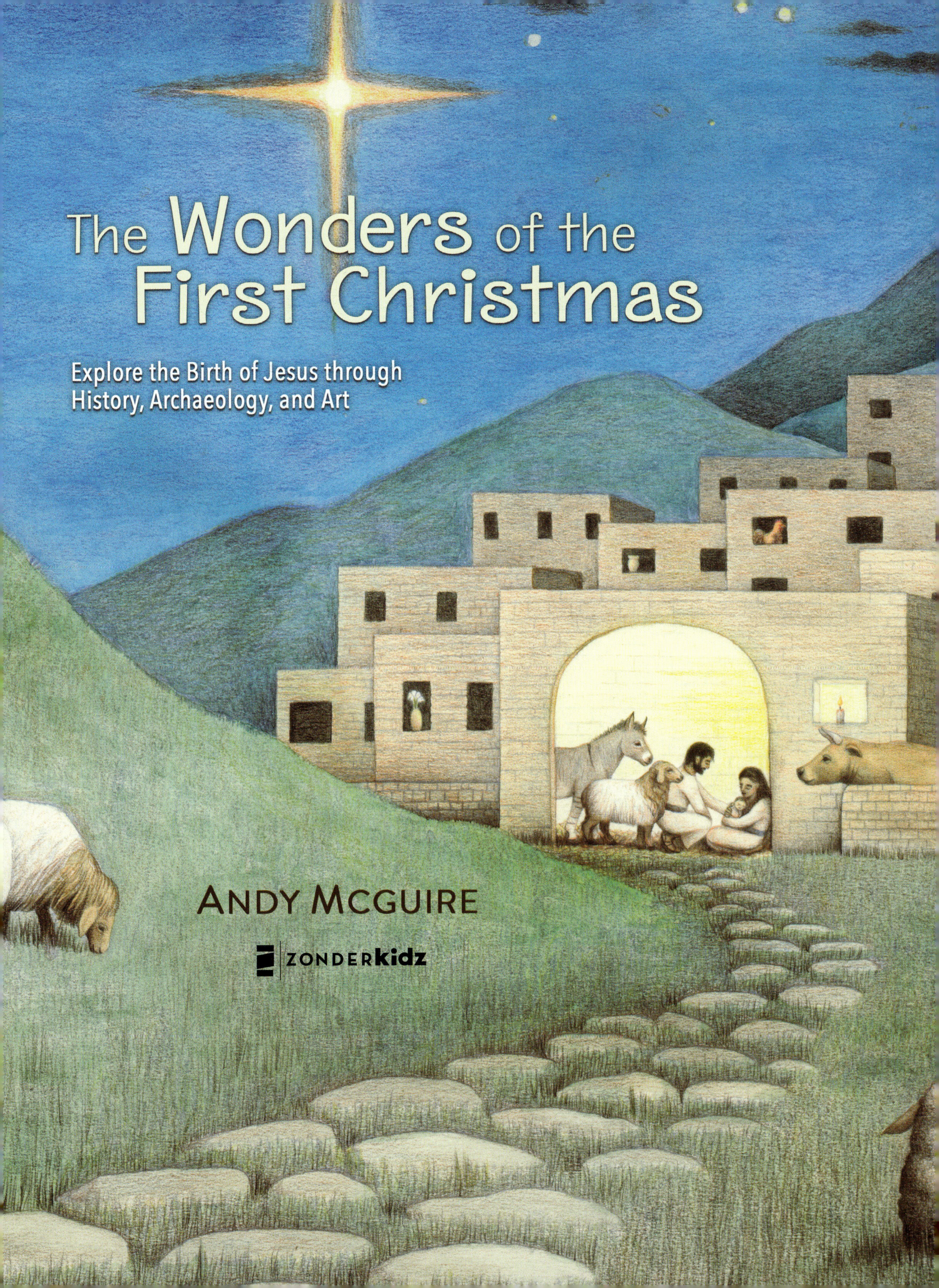

The Wonders of the First Christmas

Explore the Birth of Jesus through History, Archaeology, and Art

Andy McGuire

ZONDERkidz

ZONDERKIDZ

The Wonders of the First Christmas

Zonderkidz, 3950 Sparks Drive SE, Suite 101, Grand Rapids, Michigan 49546

Published in Grand Rapids, Michigan, by Zonderkidz. Zonderkidz is a registered trademark of The Zondervan Corporation, L.L.C., a wholly owned subsidiary of HarperCollins Christian Publishing, Inc.

Requests for information should be addressed to customercare@harpercollins.com.

ISBN 978-0-310-17021-1 (hardcover)
ISBN 978-0-310-17022-8 (ebook)

Library of Congress Cataloging-in-Publication Data
ISBN 978-0-310-17021-1

Editor: Katherine Jacobs
Illustrations: Andy McGuire
Art direction: Patti Evans
Interior Design: Emily Ghattas

Printed in Rawang, Malaysia

25 26 27 28 29 30 /VPM/ 6 5 4 3 2 1

God loved us so much that he wanted to be with us. From the very beginning he had a plan, and nothing can stop God's plans.

God sent an angel to Nazareth to tell a young woman named Mary some amazing news: She was going to have a baby, and the baby would be God's own Son.

A carpenter named Joseph had asked Mary to be his wife, so God sent an angel to him in a dream. The angel also told Joseph God's plan: Mary was going to give birth to God's Son, and they should name him Jesus.

When we picture carpenters, we think of people who work with wood. But the Bible uses the word *carpenter* more broadly to mean "builder." Most of the buildings in Bible times were made of stone, so it is likely that Joseph, and later Jesus, worked with stone more than wood and built buildings rather than things like furniture. Stones are very heavy, so it would have been hard work. Joseph must have been very strong.

Mary and Joseph lived in a country named Israel. At that time, the Roman Empire controlled Israel and many other places in the world. The Romans wanted the Israelites to pay taxes, so they made everyone go back to the cities where they were born. That way they would be easier to count.

Rome was a city in Italy with a very strong army. Soldiers on horseback and in chariots attacked and conquered surrounding cities and countries until eventually the Romans controlled the whole area around the Mediterranean Sea—a land that now includes 30 present-day countries! The Romans used concrete, which they invented, to build many roads, walls, and cities in their empire. They also built aqueducts, which were ingenious structures for carrying water to distant places.

Mary and Joseph had to walk from Nazareth to Bethlehem to be counted, a long trip made more difficult because Mary was pregnant.

The Bible doesn't say that Mary rode a donkey to Bethlehem, but many historians think she did because donkeys were a common way to get around in ancient Israel. In fact, many years later, on Palm Sunday, Jesus rode a donkey into Jerusalem. (John 12:12–15) Why donkeys? Because they have better endurance than horses and are great at handling the dry climate of the Middle East. Donkeys have a reputation for being stubborn, but they are also strong and fearless. Donkeys are ancestors of the African wild ass, which has stripes on its legs like a zebra. Every once in a while, you can see a donkey with striped legs!

When they finally got to Bethlehem, there was nowhere for Mary and Joseph to stay because all the inns were full. But God had a plan. They settled into a barn where animals lived.

God's own Son was born where people kept animals, but it might not have been the kind of stable or barn you're picturing. Back then, rather than having a separate building for animals, they were often kept somewhere in the house. People would sleep on the top floor and build a few stalls for animals on the ground floor, so the warmth from the animals could heat up their homes.

The word *inn* in the Bible is another way of saying "a room for guests." Unfortunately, when Mary and Joseph arrived in Bethlehem, all the guest rooms were filled, so the only space left was downstairs with noisy, stinky animals.

And there among the
animals, Jesus was born.

The Bible says Jesus was "wrapped in swaddling cloths and lying in a manger" (Luke 2:12 ESV). Swaddling cloths were soft cloths—probably made of linen—that were tightly wrapped around a baby to keep them calm and warm. Linen is made from a plant called flax and is smooth, soft, and strong. People still swaddle their babies today.

Out in the wild, not too far from Bethlehem, shepherds were watching their sheep. It seemed like any other ordinary, peaceful night.

Shepherds had an important job to do. People needed sheep's wool for their clothes, and they also used sheep for milk and meat. Some historians think the shepherds in the fields outside Bethlehem were working for local priests, to raise lambs for sacrificing. Shepherds weren't rich—they were just regular, hardworking people. But in the Bible, God often compares himself to a shepherd because of how they protect and guide their sheep. It was all part of his plan that shepherds were the first to worship Jesus.

The Awassi is the most common breed of sheep in Israel and the Middle East. They are usually white or cream-colored with darker heads and legs that can be brown, red, or black. They are good at handling all weather—very hot or very cold—and can live in dry places.

Sheep are easily frightened and have very little protection from their natural enemies like wolves, lions, leopards, and other meat-eaters. They need shepherds to protect them.

Suddenly, God's angel came down from heaven. He was so bright and powerful that the shepherds were terrified. But the angel said, "Don't be afraid, I've got wonderful news. A king has been born in a barn not very far away." A huge group of angels then appeared and began singing about how amazing God is and how he wants to bring peace.

After the angels left, the shepherds stared at each other in wonder. "Let's go!" they said and hurried off to Bethlehem.

In the Bible, the word *angel* means "messenger." God often uses them to give messages to people. Angels are spiritual beings—not physical beings like we are—and they can travel between heaven and earth. The Bible never talks about them having wings; in fact, they're usually described as looking like people. But almost every time they show up in the Bible, people are terrified! It can be scary to see something you don't understand.

The shepherds hurried to Bethlehem where they found the baby Jesus in a manger. The angels' wonderful news was true!

To make a manger, people would hollow out a large stone and put animal food in it. In other words, it is likely that Jesus was put in a big, rock bowl with animals nibbling straw all around him. What a surprising place to find God's Son!

Meanwhile, far away to the east of Israel, wise men who studied the nighttime sky saw a brand-new star appear. God put it there as part of his plan to tell them that a powerful king was born in Israel.

So they set out to find him by following that star.

The Bible doesn't say where these men came from, but many people believe they were from Persia, in modern-day Iran. The Persians had conquered Israel many years before, capturing prisoners and taking them back to their lands. One of the prisoners was Daniel, and while he was there in Babylon he prophesied about a good and powerful king who would rule the world. This too was part of God's plan. He wanted people all over the world to know about Jesus.

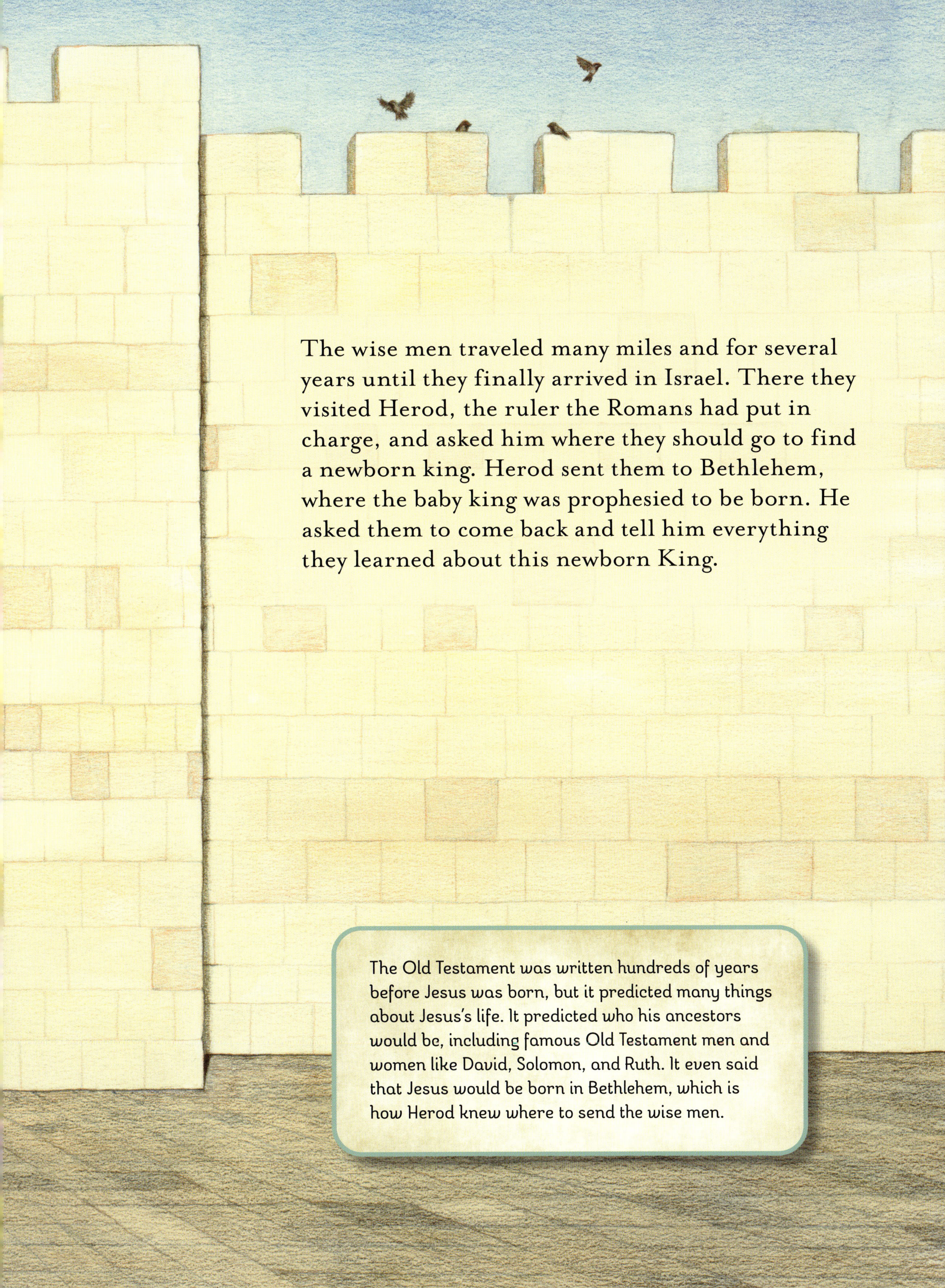

The wise men traveled many miles and for several years until they finally arrived in Israel. There they visited Herod, the ruler the Romans had put in charge, and asked him where they should go to find a newborn king. Herod sent them to Bethlehem, where the baby king was prophesied to be born. He asked them to come back and tell him everything they learned about this newborn King.

The Old Testament was written hundreds of years before Jesus was born, but it predicted many things about Jesus's life. It predicted who his ancestors would be, including famous Old Testament men and women like David, Solomon, and Ruth. It even said that Jesus would be born in Bethlehem, which is how Herod knew where to send the wise men.

The wise men continued to follow the star and it led them to Bethlehem, just like Herod had advised. They found Jesus and worshiped him, giving him rare and expensive presents—gold, frankincense, and myrrh.

People who study the Bible believe that the wise men visited Jesus when he was a little older than a baby—he may have been two or three years old. The Bible tells us they brought him gold, frankincense, and myrrh. In those days *gold* probably meant gold coins, and *frankincense* and *myrrh* were both expensive perfumes. They were most likely presented to him in fancy, beautiful containers. These types of presents sound a little strange to us, but they were very good gifts to give a king!

After the wise men visited Jesus, God warned them in a dream not to go back to Herod. Secretly, Herod wanted to kill this baby king because he wanted to be the only leader in Israel. So the wise men took the long way home and never saw the evil ruler of Israel again.

The Bible doesn't mention the wise men riding camels, but they were a common way for people to travel over the huge deserts between Persia and Israel. Camels are perfect for desert travel, since they can go weeks without food or water. When they finally find water, they can drink up to twenty-five gallons in ten minutes! They don't mind hot temperatures and only sweat if it's above 105 degrees.

Herod didn't give up so easily. He still wanted to kill Jesus, so God warned Joseph about Herod's plans. Joseph took his young family and ran away to Egypt. They didn't come back to Israel until God told Joseph in another dream that it was safe to return.

Egypt is a large country south and west of Israel, in the northeastern corner of Africa. Like Israel, Egypt was under Roman rule, but it wasn't under the control of Herod, who was only in charge of Israel. Egypt was a great trading partner with Israel and many other countries. They built huge pyramids used as tombs and were one of the most advanced civilizations in the world at that time. We still use some of their inventions like toothbrushes, wigs, and the game of bowling today!

At last Mary, Joseph, and Jesus made it back home to Bethlehem, safe and sound. God's only Son could fulfill his purpose and bring us to God.

God's plan worked, like it always does.

Sea of Galilee
This way to Persia
Mediterranean Sea
Nazareth
Jordan River
Jerusalem
Bethlehem
Dead Sea
Mt. Sinai *
*Estimated location

Bibliography

Clutton-Brock, Juliet. *Eyewitness: Horse.* 1992, DK. Pages 16–17, 24–25.

Cobble, Tara-Leigh. *The Bible Recap.* 2020, Bethany House Publishers. Pages 568–571.

Croteau, David. "Christmas Urban Legends: Shepherds as Outcasts." Lifeway Research. https://research.lifeway.com/2015/12/17/christmas-urban-legends-shepherds-as-outcasts/. Accessed 2/25/24.

Darling, Daniel. "Nobodies Were the First to Know." *Christianity Today*; excerpted from The Characters of Christmas: The Unlikely People Caught Up in the Story of Jesus (Moody, 2019) https://www.christianitytoday.com/2019/12/characters-christmas-daniel-darling-shepherds/. Accessed 2/25/24.

Dubois, Muriel L. *Ancient Rome: A Mighty Empire.* 2012, Capstone Press.

Gallaty, Robby. "The Forgotten Jesus Part 2: Was Jesus a Carpenter or a Stonemason?" Lifeway Leadership. https://leadership.lifeway.com/2017/04/04/the-forgotten-jesus-part-2-was-jesus-a-carpenter-or-a-stonemason/. Accessed 2/25/24.

Hart, George. *Eyewitness Ancient Egypt.* 2014, DK. Page 8.

Hayhurst, Susan. "Donkeys: The Epitome of Stubborn." https://www.farmprogress.com/commentary/donkeys-the-epitome-of-stubborn. Accessed 2/25/24.

Horses and Ponies. 2021, DK. Page 15.

Leighton, Christina. *Animals on the Farm: Sheep.* 2018, Bellweather Media.

Malam, John. *Ancient Rome Inside Out.* 2017, Crabtree Publishing.

Manning, Gary Jr. "What Are Swaddling Clothes?" Biola.edu. https://www.biola.edu/blogs/good-book-blog/2021/what-are-swaddling-clothes. Accessed 2/25/24.

Reynolds, Donna. *Ancient Egypt Revealed.* 2023, Cavendish Square. Page 5.

Roat, Alyssa. "Who Were the Three Wise Men of the Christmas Story?" Christianity.com. https://www.christianity.com/wiki/holidays/who-were-the-wise-men-of-the-christmas-story.html. Accessed 2/25/24.

Sappington, Thomas. "The Spirit World: Angels." The Gospel Coalition. https://www.thegospelcoalition.org/essay/the-spirit-world-angels/. Accessed 2/25/24.

"Sheep: Domesticated Animal." Written and fact-checked by the editors of Encyclopedia Britannica. https://www.britannica.com/animal/domesticated-sheep. Accessed 2/25/24.

Vilardi, Debbie. *Why Do Camels Have Humps?* 2019, Pop! Page 19.

"Was Jesus Born in a Cave?" Adapted from *The Life of Our Lord Upon the Earth* by Samuel James Andrews. Christianity.com. https://www.christianity.com/jesus/birth-of-jesus/bethlehem/was-jesus-born-in-a-cave.html. Accessed 2/25/24.

"What Does the Bible Say about Angels and Cherubim?" Cheree Hayes and the BibleProject Team. Thebibleproject.com. https://bibleproject.com/articles/what-does-the-bible-say-about-angels-and-cherubim/. Accessed 2/25/24.

"What Does the Bible Say about the Three Wise Men (Magi)." Gotquestions.org. https://www.gotquestions.org/three-wise-men.html. Accessed 2/25/24.

Zeigler, Jennifer. *Camels.* 2015, Children's Press. Pages 9, 10, 13.